# Kaizen

## Lean Thinking Series

## SUMEET SAVANT

# DEDICATION

To all Lean Six Sigma enthusiasts, practitioners, and professionals.

# CONTENTS

# ACKNOWLEDGMENTS

Special thanks to my wife Sahana, for always supporting me in all my endeavors and to the world of Lean Six Sigma for accepting and enabling me to perform at a global scale.

# ABOUT THE AUTHOR

Sumeet Savant is a Lean Six Sigma Master Black Belt Mentor and coach, with more than a decade of experience in executing, leading and mentoring Lean Six Sigma process improvement projects. He is a BTech, MBA, and Prince certified Practitioner. He has facilitated hundreds of process improvement projects, and coached hundreds of professionals, Yellow, Green, and Black Belts over the years. He lives in Mumbai, India with his family.

# LEAN

# LEAN, VALUE, AND WASTE

**Lean** is now a common term, synonymous with process improvement, waste elimination and cost reduction.

You probably might have heard about Lean, or might have some basic idea about Lean, or might be even working on and practicing Lean methodologies

Before we start, let us understand what the term Lean really means.

Formally defined, "**Lean** is a continuous improvement strategy, focused on **maximizing customer value**, by **minimizing waste** in all the business processes, or products."

So, now the question arises, what do the terms Value and Waste mean.

"**Value**, means something, that the customer is willing to pay for, extending this definition, we can say it is something which the customer **needs, and hence expects**, from the product or service, for which he buys it.".

And, by "**Waste** we mean, any activity or feature that **does not add value** to the product or service, from the point of view of the customer."

The Japanese term for Waste so defined, is **Muda**.

Some of the examples of Waste or Muda are,

• Unnecessary travel like driving, or riding.

• Waiting for approval.

• Unnecessary Movement like bending, or stretching.

• Producing more than required.

Though Lean is primarily focused on reduction of waste, the Lean strategies framework is much broader.

To understand the Lean framework, it is a must to be well acquainted with something that is known as the **House of Lean**.

.

# HOUSE OF LEAN

The collection of Lean concepts, practices, and tools, put together in a container that looks like a home, to act as a framework for implementing a complete Lean system is known as the **House of Lean.**

## House of Lean: Goals

The first component of House of Lean is its roof, which represents the **Goals** of the business.

Most businesses have similar goals as follows,

• **Highest Quality**

Quality in terms of features and characteristics of the products or services provided to the customer.

• **Lowest Cost**

Lowest cost in terms of raw materials, man power, and machinery required to design, develop and deliver the products.

• **Shortest Lead Time**

Shortest time taken from initiation of idea to going to market of the products or services.

The roof of the House of quality is depicted in the following figure.

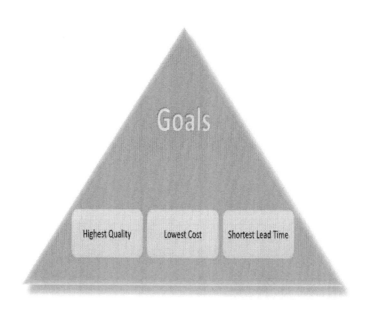

## House of Lean: JIT

The next component of the House of Lean is its left pillar, which represents the **JIT or Just In Time** concepts, practices, and tools.

## Just In Time

JIT is a methodology aimed primarily at reducing flow times within production system as well as response times from suppliers and to customers. It aims at reducing the inventory, and overproduction by producing just in time to meet the customer demands.

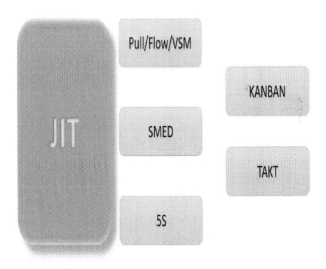

The JIT concepts, practices, and tools include the following,

• **Pull**

Pull means producing to the customer demand.

• **Flow**

In Lean, the process flow, which means to move along in a steady, continuous stream, should be free of waste, and issues, to ensure a steady continuous uninterrupted flow.

• **VSM**

Value Stream Mapping is a technique to chart the flow of the processes, identify wastes in the flow, establishing root causes for the wastes, and identifying ways to reduce or eliminate the wastes.

• **KANBAN**

Kanban is a scheduling system for lean manufacturing and just-in-time manufacturing, that makes use of cards to track, schedule and control production.

• **SMED**

Single-minute exchange of die, is a lean production method to provide a rapid and efficient way of converting a manufacturing process from running the current product to running the next product, it is a system for reducing the time taken for equipment changeovers.

• **TAKT**

TAKT Time, is the average time or rate at which a product needs to be completed in order to meet customer demand.

**• 5S**

5S is a workplace organization framework that uses five Japanese words to represent its principles or phases: Seiri(Sort), Seiton(Set in order), Seiso(Shine), Seiketsu(Standardize), and Shitsuke(Sustain).

## House of Lean: JIDOKA

The next component of the House of Lean is its right pillar, which represents the **JIDOKA** concepts, practices, and tools.

## JIDOKA

JIDOKA, also known as Autonomation which means "Intelligent Automation" or "Humanized Automation", is an automation which implements some sort of monitory techniques, making it "aware" enough to detect an abnormal situation, and stop the machine, to enable the workers to stop the production line, investigate the root causes and fix the issue.

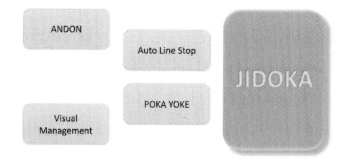

The JIDOKA concepts, practices, and tools include the following,

## • ANDON

ANDON is an alerting system that notifies management, maintenance, and other workers of a quality or process problem. It can be manual or automated.

## • Auto Line Stop

Auto Line Stop is a system that stops the production process whenever an issue or defect occurs, it can be automated or manual.

## • POKA YOKE

POKA YOKE or Mistake Proofing, is a lean mechanism that helps an equipment operator avoid (yokeru) mistakes (poka). It eliminates product defects by preventing, correcting, or drawing attention to human errors as they occur.

## • Visual Management

Visual Management is a lean system to manage production and processes through visual signs and controls.

.

## House of Lean: Standardization and Stability

The next component of the House of Lean is its strong base, which represents the **Standardization and Stability** concepts, practices, and tools.

### Standardization and Stability

Standardization and Stability, deal with standardizing the work, processes, and workplace, with an aim to consistently achieve the best, and with stabilizing the processes to avoid fluctuations and variations in output.

The Standardization and Stability concepts, practices, and

tools include the following,

**• Standardized Work**

Standardized Work is a work derived from best practices and lessons learned while performing the work, to do it in a most efficient way, to improve productivity and avoid rework.

**• HEIJUNKA**

HEIJUNKA or leveling, is a technique to level the work or production load to reduce unevenness or Mura.

**• KAIZEN**

KAIZEN is a continuous improvement approach based on the idea that small, continuous or consistent positive changes can reap major improvements.

## House of Lean: Respect for Individual

The final and core component of the House of Lean is to establish the values of **Respect for Individual**.

### Respect for Individual

Respect for Individual, deals with empowering, motivating, and supporting the workforce to effectively and consistently participate in lean methodologies to guarantee and sustain improvements.

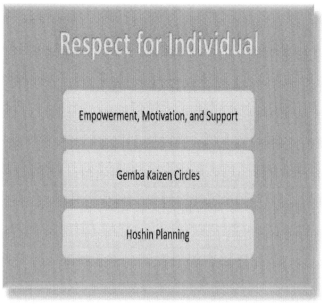

The Respect for Individual concepts, practices, and tools include the following,

## • Empowerment, Motivation, and Support

Empowerment, Motivation, and Support is a management philosophy and ideology to empower, motivate, and support the workforce to encourage them identify the areas for improvement, and participate consistently and willingly without the need to be told to do so.

## • Gemba Kaizen Circles

Gemba Kaizen is a Japanese concept of continuous improvement designed for enhancing processes and reducing waste at the workplace including the workforce, or the people that work at the location. Gemba refers to the location where value is created, while Kaizen relates to improvements.

## • HOSHIN Planning

HOSHIN Planning is a strategic planning process in which strategic goals are communicated throughout the company and then put into action.

## House of Lean

With all the components combined, the House of Lean looks similar to the following depicted figure.

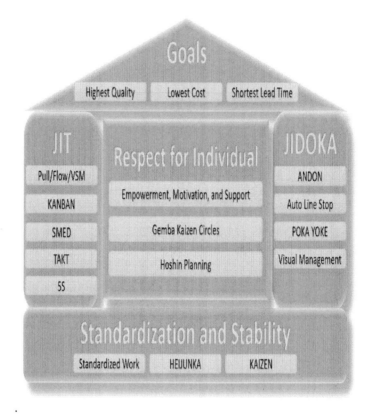

# FIVE PRINCIPLES OF LEAN

There are five principles of lean, based around customer, values, quality and wastes. They are,

## Define Value

To be able to understand the first principle of Lean, it is essential to know what "Value" and "Quality" are.

**Value** is something that the customer is willing to pay for. It is something that the customer expects from the product or service, he buys. It is something, which satisfies the customer's needs.

**Quality** of a product or service is the degree of value the product or service adds to the customer. It means, the degree to which the product or service satisfies the customer's needs

For a company to survive and succeed, it is essential that it understands the needs of its customers, and how its products and services can satisfy its customer's needs by providing the right quality and adding the right value.

So, it is very essential to identify and define value from the point of view of the customer, and produce products and services that deliver maximum quality, and value.

Due to this reason, the very first principle in lean states to define or identify value from the point of view of the customer.

What is valuable to customer, or what are the customer's needs can be found out by collecting the VOC or the **Voice of customer**.

There are many ways VOC can be gathered, such as interviews, surveys, and market and web analytics that can help you discover what customers seek value in.

## Map Value Stream

Once you identify what the customer values in your products or services, the next step is to understand the steps and activities involved in creating the value.

The **Value stream** is the complete end to end flow of a product's life-cycle.

It starts from the getting the raw materials used to make the product, and goes on up to the customer's buying, using, and ultimately disposing of the product.

**Mapping the Value Stream**, in this context, is an exercise to create a flowchart or a process map of all the activities involved in the product's complete life cycle.

The **Value stream process map** thus created outlines each and every step of the process for each part of the business, right from market research, to R&D, to Design, to Development, to Production, to Marketing, to Sales and Services, etc.

Only by thoroughly studying and understanding the value stream can a company understand the wastes associated, and hence find opportunities to reduce costs and tackle issues, in manufacturing and delivery of a product or service.

Supplier and customer partnership is one of the core ideas of Lean as it helps understand the complete supply chain, and eliminate wastes and other issues from the entire value stream.

## Create Flow

Once you have the Value Stream Map ready, the next step will be to create Flow.

To **Create Flow**, means to ensure that the flow of the process steps is smooth and free of interruptions or delays.

The first action to achieve this is to analyze the process map for wastes.

Once the wastes are analyzed, you can perform root cause analysis to understand the causes behind the wastes.

These causes needs to be acted upon to ensure the flow of steps and activities are smoothed and made free of any issues, problems, or bottlenecks.

Once the wastes are eliminated, you can find further ways to maximize efficiencies.

Some strategies for ensuring smooth flow include breaking down steps, re-engineering the steps, work and production leveling, creating cross-functional and multi-skilled departments, suppliers, and workforce.

## Establish Pull

Once you have eliminated the wastes in the process, and created the flow, the next step would be to establish Pull.

**Pull** is producing as per customer demand.

Inventory and Overproduction are two of the most problematic wastes in any production systems.

The ultimate goal of the pull system is to limit stocking up the inventory, and to produce only to meet the customer demand

To achieve this, you need to effectively look at the operations of the business in reverse on the value stream maps.

The idea is to capture and analyze the exact moments as to when the customers actually need the product.

This helps to implement the JIT mode of manufacturing and operations where products are produced just in time when the customers need them.

Extending this further, this also helps to get and procure even the raw materials, just in time when the production needs them.

## Pursue Perfection

Once you have eliminated the wastes in the process, created the flow, and established the Pull, the final step is to keep the improvements sustained, and ongoing.

Perfection is to achieve the absolute best in anything that the company does.

So, it is absolutely not enough to just eliminate wastes, create flow, and establish pull.

You need to develop a mindset of continual improvement.

Each and every employee should strive towards perfection, and work with an aim to deliver consistent value.

This relentless pursuit of perfection is key attitude of an organization that is "going for lean", and makes Lean thinking and continuous process improvement a part of the organizational culture.

The following figure depicts the five principles of Lean.

# WASTES

# TYPES OF WORK

Before we can understand what waste is, it is very important to understand what are the types of work.

There are three types of work based on the customer's point of view, as to how the customer looks at the work done.

They are,

• **Value Added Work**

• **Business Necessary Work**

• **Non Value Added Work**

Now, we will see each of these work types in detail.

## Value Added Work

**Value Added Work** is the first type of work activity.

It is type of activity or work, for which the customer is willing to pay for.

Any activity which the customer perceives as actually adding value to the product or service is termed as **Value Added Work**.

These activities have the following characteristics which classify these activities as value adding.

### • Change/Transformation

These activities change or transform an item from one condition to another, or from one state to another, with an overall focus of reaching the final state of the product or service, which the customer needs.

### • First Time Right

These activities are done in a right way, or correctly the very first time, that is without the need for corrections or rework.

### • Customer is willing to pay

These activities are activities which the customer wants done, as he perceives them to be necessary steps to create the product or service he expects, and hence is willing to pay for.

## Business Necessary Work

**Business Necessary Work** is the second type of work activity.

It is type of activity or work, for which though the customer is unwilling to pay, still needs to be performed to create the product or services the customer needs.

This type of activity may have similar characteristics as Value Adding Activity like, transformation of an item from one state to another, or done correctly the first time.

However, the important difference which classify this type of activity differently is that the customer does not care for this activity, and hence is unwilling to pay.

Such work includes any work that might be performed to protect the business, or to comply with established policies or standards, or even as precautionary measures.

This type of work is also known as the following,

• **Business Value Added Work.**

• **Value Enabling Work.**

• **Necessary Non Value Added Work.**

## Non Value Added Work

**Non Value Added Work** is the third type of work activity.

This work activity adds absolutely no value to the product or service.

This work activity neither transforms nor helps in achieving the end product or service.

And most importantly, the customer is not willing to pay for this work activity.

This work activity is referred to as waste, or the **Muda** in Japanese.

To figure out any non value activity in your products or service, it is best to look at them from the point of view of customer, and think whether the customer would be willing to pay for the activity.

Lean focuses on eliminating waste, by reducing or removing the non value activities from the value stream.

## Example

Imagine you need to travel from one city to another, on a road.

Traveling on the road represents the value flow, as it helps you reach your destination.

Value added work would be you driving a vehicle on that road to reach your destination.

Non Value added work would be any additional turns, stops, and interruptions you may have to take while driving due to various reasons like traffic, broken pathways, pedestrians crossing roads etc.

Business Value added work would be any additional turns, stops interruptions you may have to take while driving due to the road and traffic rules like the zebra crossing, traffic lights, etc.

.

# NEED TO REMOVE WASTES

Before we proceed any further, let us quickly look at a visual representation that will help you understand how important it is to remove waste from our services and products.

Consider a process, a typical process will have certain value added activities, and certain non value added activities.

Following is a depiction of a value stream of such a typical process.

Value added work is depicted in green, and non value added work in red.

This may appear quite normal, and acceptable, however just wait and watch, what happens when we analyze it.

Looking at the value stream map, we may think that it depicted a normal acceptable waste presence.

However, let us now split, and separate the value added work from the non value added work.

Now look at the newly arranged value stream map, depicted in the following figure.

You will get to clearly see what the wastes are doing to our processes.

As you can see, the minor wastes hidden here and there when taken together do appear huge, and sometimes huge enough to harm the process.

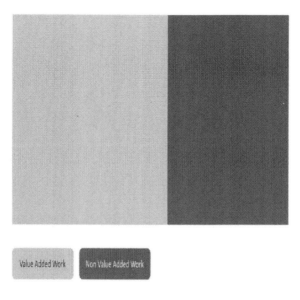

Value Added Work    Non Value Added Work

Let us continue the analysis one more step further.

Let us now actually calculate the percentage distribution of the value added and the non value added work or activity in our process.

And then let us plot the distribution in a pie chart, to get a visual feel of the percentage distribution.

Depicted below is the figure of pie distribution so created.

If you see, the total waste in our process is 43%, with so much waste hidden in our processes no wonder they are so costly.

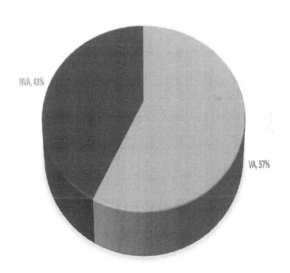

PERCENTAGE DISTRIBUTION

NVA, 43%

VA, 57%

VA  NVA

Lean focuses on saving these costs, by eliminating wastes and improving processes.

Imagine that the total time taken by our process is 2000 person hours, and per hour uniform cost of 50 USD.

So, the total cost of our process then would be 100000 USD

And, since 43% of the time was going waste,

The process clearly wasted as much as 860 person hour per run, and a dollar wastage of 43000 USD

If we now consider that this process runs just even once per day, just imagine the kind of loss this process is creating annually.

The reason why Lean is so powerful is that it focuses on searching such opportunities where costs can be saved.

And, as we have seen so far, to achieve the highest cost reductions in our processes, it is imperative that we need to hunt for wastes in them.

And, to hunt for wastes, we need to have a clear understanding of what the wastes are, their types, and how we can control and eliminate them.

# THE 3 M'S

Any discussion on wastes, will be incomplete if we do not talk about the 3 infamous M's in the Lean world, the Muda, Muri, and Mura.

## Muda

**Muda** in Japanese means useless, or waste, and comes in eight forms.

The figure below clearly depicts Muda, as can be seen, the truck is not being utilized to its fullest capacity, and hence considerable space is being **wasted**.

## Muri

**Muri** is the overloading or overburdening of employees, or machines, or processes.

Employees, machines, and even processes, have thresholds or limits, which should be respected.

Trying to get more done from them, beyond their capacity, can lead to break downs or stress, and low morale.

The figure below clearly depicts Muri, as can be seen, the truck is overloaded to the point of tipping or loosing balance.

Establishing TAKT time, standardizing work, and implementing pull systems are some of the ways to avoid Muri.

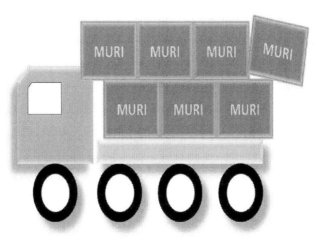

## Mura

**Mura** is the unevenness or fluctuation or variation in the work, or workplace.

We often see this in products and services due to rushed delivery, or poor planning.

Establishing TAKT time, leveling work (Heijunka), implementing Six Sigma and pull systems are some of the ways to avoid Mura.

The figure below clearly depicts Mura, as can be seen, the two carriages of the truck are unevenly loaded.

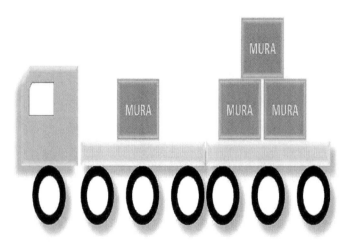

UNEVENNESS

## The Ideal State

**No Muda, No Muri, and No Mura** is the ideal state to be achieved and sustained in any lean system.

Processes should be free or wastes, overloading, and unevenness or variation.

The figure below clearly depicts a No Muda, Muri, Mura state, as can be seen, the truck is carrying just the ideal load, free of the 3 M's.

NO MUDA, NO MURI, NO MURA

# KAIZEN

# KAIZEN

Lean as we saw earlier, is focused on reducing wastes, costs and continually improving the quality and hence the value of the processes and products of any business.

**Kaizen**, is one of the key components and the most effective methodology that helps keep up the focus of continuous improvement in Lean.

**Kaizen** in Japanese is made up of two terms, **Kai** and **Zen**.

**Kai** in Japanese means change, or reform, or improve.

**Zen** in Japanese means good.

So, together **Kai + Zen** becomes **Kaizen**, which in Japanese means improvement.

Hence **Kaizen**, stands for change for good, or a good change.

The following figure clearly depicts the term Kaizen, for a better understanding.

# Kaizen

## 改善

## Kai + Zen

## Change + Good

## Good Change
## Or Change for good
## Or Continuous Improvement

# NEED FOR KAIZEN

Most often processes have a tendency to degrade in performance over time.

Lean Six Sigma projects do help in improving the processes drastically, however even the improved processes tend to degrade in performance over time.

And the cycle continues, of degradation and drastic improvements.

Continuous improvement tries to prevent this degradation by continuously focusing on implementing minor improvements.

This is where Kaizen fits in perfectly. Kaizen can be thought of as PDCA cycles where minor improvements are continuously implemented every cycle.

The net result is that your processes never degrade and continue to perform efficiently and effectively.

The following figure clearly depicts the need for Kaizen.

As can be seen with Kaizen there is no scope for process performance degradation, instead it keeps continuously improving, which is what every business should strive for.

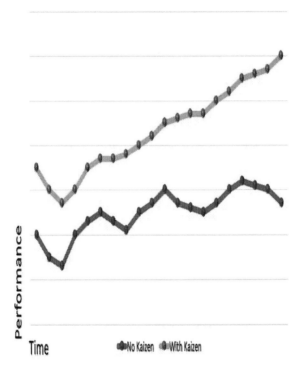

# KAIZEN, LEAN AND SIX SIGMA

Most often Six Sigma projects like DMAIC, DMADV take months and a huge amount of study to complete successfully, often times resulting in drastic savings.

Lean, on the other hand take lesser times as the study and effort involved is relatively less. However, Lean projects also often times result in drastic savings.

Lean, and Six Sigma are the kind of improvement projects that aim for major improvements, often times impacting multiple process areas, and taking much time, which is why they are executed less frequently.

So, what do we do to keep continuously improving?.

As mentioned earlier, this is where Kaizen fits in pretty well. Kaizen are similar to PDCA cycles where minor improvements are continuously implemented every cycle which lasts around a week.

The following figure clearly depicts the positioning of Kaizen improvements against Lean and Six Sigma, in terms of efforts and time needed for complete end to end implementation.

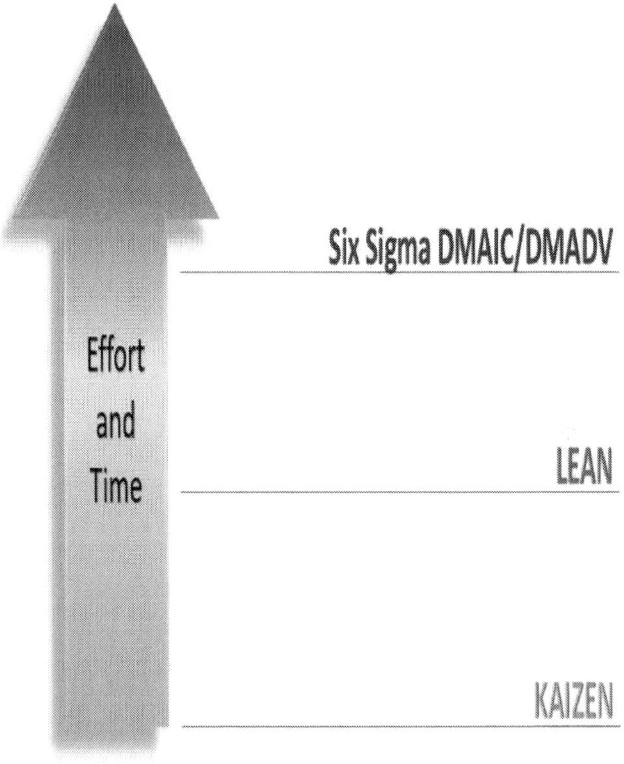

# WHEN TO USE KAIZEN

Kaizen as we have seen so far are the kind of improvements that are minor and continuous in nature.

Kaizen can best used, when you have a

• **Well understood problem,** Kaizen as we know are quick continuous improvements, and for any improvement to be quick, you first need to have a thorough understanding of the problem. If you do not know the problem, you often times need to do a lot of study over the problem, which would then call for core Six Sigma like DMAIC, and DMADV projects instead. So, any problems on which you have a clear understanding are best opportunities for executing Kaizen.

**• Recurring issues which need same fix every time,** Kaizen as we have understood are similar to PDCA projects, which often times aim at fixing known problems. So, if you have recurring issues where you end up implementing the same solution again and again, it is best to proactively find out such opportunities in your processes and products and execute Kaizen projects on them.

**• Solution that needs minimal effort,** When you know the solutions for problems, or you have a good idea about how the solution should be designed, and implemented, then such problems are excellent opportunities to implement Kaizen. It is best to execute Kaizen on problems that have straight forward, simple, and logical solutions, which will need the least of study and analysis.

• **Problems that need immediate fixes,** Most often problems need immediate fixes, and if such problems can be clearly understood, and have known or straight forward logical solutions, and result in continuous improvements, then such problems are again excellent opportunities to implement Kaizen.

• **Solutions for which risks are minimal,** Often times implementing solutions can pose risks, like side effects, or undue impacts. The solutions for problems that pose the least or most minimal risks are often times the best opportunities to implement Kaizen.

• **Resistance to change,** Often times new solutions do face resistance from the users, who have got used to the old ways of doing things. Kaizen projects are excellent in such cases, as the new solutions can act as change agents to positively influence such resistors.

• **Resource limitations,** Often times it is not feasible to implement a long term solution. Chances might arise where there are simply not enough resources, or even budget. In such cases Kaizen can play an important role for implementing improvements in increments to reach the desired final long term solution.

The figure below shows when Kaizen can be utilized or used, for a better understanding.

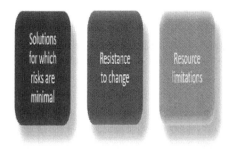

# KEY PRINCIPLES OF KAIZEN

Kaizen is a continuous improvement framework, and often relies on following principles to succeed.

**• Small or incremental improvements,** Kaizen focuses on keeping the improvements small, or minor, to be able to deliver or implement faster. Since Kaizen helps in ensuring continuous improvements it necessarily tries to implement improvements in increments of smaller packages, instead of a big bang or huge implementations.

**• Implement improvements frequently,** Kaizen focuses to establish a practice of continuously improving processes or products. Hence it deliberately focuses on implementing minor changes at a fixed frequency, instead of implementing some big change once in a blue moon, and then forgetting it. The frequency can be monthly, weekly, or even as high as daily improvements.

• **Waste reduction and cost leadership,** Kaizen helps everyone understand and recognize that there is always a room for improvement. It helps develop a mindset to continuously identify wastes everywhere and achieve cost leadership.

• **Complete workforce participation,** Kaizen empowers and encourages each and every employee or worker of the workforce to participate, suggest, and implement improvements. Participation is a critical component of Kaizen. Kaizen believes in encouraging and enabling people to participate in process improvement instead of forcing them to do so.

- **Workplace Improvement or Gemba Kaizen,**
Kaizen also focuses to continuously improve the Gemba, or the workplace, where the actual work happens on day to day basis. This ensures to continuously improve the processes, the organization, and the people of the Gemba, to make the entire organization lean.

- **Humanized Improvements,** Kaizen also focuses on motivating the workforce by making processes simpler and easier, by reducing and leveling work, and reducing unnecessary stress and strain. And the beauty of it is that Kaizen empowers the workforce to come up with improvements to make their own lives easy, work fulfilling, and work area safe and clean.

• **Disciplined Improvements,** Kaizen by itself is a highly disciplined method that ensures continuous improvements in business work processes, work place, and work force. As it focuses on creating improvements in increments, at a regular frequency, ensuring everyone participates, and achieve overall business effectiveness and efficiency, by reducing wastes and costs.

The figure below the Kaizen principles for ensuring continuous improvements.

# CLASSIFICATION OF KAIZEN

Kaizen which focuses on continuous improvements can be classified broadly into two types based on the approach.

This kind of classification is based on the measure of implementing continuous improvements.

The classification is based on the interpretations of the word Kaizen which means continuous improvements, and are frequently used in the context of modern management discussions.

They are,

- **Flow Kaizen**.
- **Process Kaizen**.

## Flow Kaizen

Flow Kaizen is often oriented towards the flow of materials and information, and is often identified with the reorganization of an entire production area, often times even a business.

These improvements are directed towards the entire value streams, and hence can include all processes, and process areas involved in creation of value.

Such improvements often make use of Kaizen events or work shops.

And may take about a few weeks, most times anywhere between two to four weeks.

## Process Kaizen

Process Kaizen on the other hand is often oriented towards individual work stands, or work stations, or work areas.

These improvements are directed towards individual processes, and hence are usually limited to single processes or sub process of a value stream.

Such improvements often make use of Kaizen blitz and super blitz.

And may take about a few days, most times anywhere between two to five days.

The figure below depicts the classification of Kaizen based on approach, for better understanding.

* Improvements across entire Value streams.
* Kaizen events or workshops.
* 2 to 5 weeks.

* Improvements across individual processes of Value streams.
* Kaizen blitz.
* 2 to 5 days.

# THE 4 K'S OF LEAN

Any discussion on Kaizen, will be incomplete if we do not talk about the 4 famous K's in the Lean world.

They are,

- **The Kaizen**.

- **The Kaikaku**.

- **The Kakushin**.

And finally we have,

- **The Kairyo**.

# Kaizen

Kaizen is the small incremental improvements the business, especially its workforce keep on doing to achieve continuous improvements.

By necessity Kaizen most often are,

• Small changes.

• Incremental in nature.

• Frequent, and continuous.

• Driven by people or workforce, often times for workforce.

• Focused on waste reduction in processes.

• Analogous to PDCA improvements.

## Kaikaku

Kaikaku is the radical change the business, often does to achieve revolutionary improvements.

By necessity Kaikaku most often are,

• Radical changes to existing situations.

• Revolutionary in nature.

• Continuous, though less frequent.

• Driven by businesses for drastic improvements.

• Focused on upgrading existing processes and products.

• Analogous to DMAIC improvements.

## Kaikushin

Kaikushin is the transformation change the business, often does to achieve innovative improvements.
By necessity Kaikushin most often are,

• Complete change from existing situations.

• Innovative in nature.

• Non continuous, not frequent.

• Driven by businesses for reformative improvements.

• Focused on replacing existing processes and products.

• Analogous to DMADV improvements.

## Kairyo

Kairyo is similar to Kaizen, however with a major difference that, where Kaizen strives to achieve incremental improvements through internal people and mindset, Kairyo strives to achieve the same through external investments.

By necessity Kairyo most often are,

• Major changes.

• Drastic in nature.

• Less Frequent, yet continuous.

• Driven using external investments and techniques.

• Focused on major technical improvements in processes.

The figure below depicts the 4 K's of Lean, for better understanding.

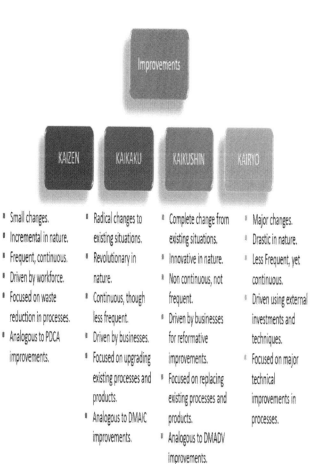

**KAIZEN**
- Small changes.
- Incremental in nature.
- Frequent, continuous.
- Driven by workforce.
- Focused on waste reduction in processes.
- Analogous to PDCA improvements.

**KAIKAKU**
- Radical changes to existing situations.
- Revolutionary in nature.
- Continuous, though less frequent.
- Driven by businesses.
- Focused on upgrading existing processes and products.
- Analogous to DMAIC improvements.

**KAIKUSHIN**
- Complete change from existing situations.
- Innovative in nature.
- Non continuous, not frequent.
- Driven by businesses for reformative improvements.
- Focused on replacing existing processes and products.
- Analogous to DMADV improvements.

**KAIRYO**
- Major changes.
- Drastic in nature.
- Less Frequent, yet continuous.
- Driven using external investments and techniques.
- Focused on major technical improvements in processes.

# TYPES OF KAIZEN ACTIVITIES

Kaizen as we know are small incremental improvements carried out within a business.

Kaizen activities are the exercises using which Kaizen is put to work to achieve continuous improvements.

These exercises are classified based on the scope planned for improvement, most often in terms of the number of days or efforts.

Kaizen activities are often classified as,

• **Kaizen Workshop**.

• **Kaizen Event**.

• **Kaizen Blitz**.

• **Kaizen Super Blitz**.

## Kaizen Workshops

Kaizen Workshops are often times a group exercise in which most of the workforce, and often times the management and leaders come together, and participate to establish goals and plans to implement improvements in multiple areas of the business.

Kaizen Workshops often times,

• Are group exercises involving workforce and management.

• Take somewhere between 5 to 7 days.

• Focus on establishing goals and plans to implement improvements.

• May involve significant study and analysis of problems and solutions.

• Establish goals oriented around multiple processes or areas.

• Focus on different aspects of the business.

## Kaizen Events

Kaizen Events are often times a group exercise in which most of the workforce, and often times the management and leaders come together, and participate, to implement improvements in single area of the business.

Kaizen Events most often,

• Are group exercises involving workforce and management.

• Take somewhere around 5 days.

• Focus on identifying and implementing significant process improvements.

• May involve significant study and analysis of problems and solutions.

• Have goals oriented around a single process or area.

• Look at a particular issue to implement improvements.

## Kaizen Blitz

Kaizen Blitz are often times individual or group exercises to implement improvements on specific issues of the business.

Kaizen Blitz often times,

• Are individual or group exercises involving workforce and management.

• Take somewhere around 2 to 5 days.

• Focus on identifying and implementing minor process improvements.

• May involve some amount of study and analysis of problems and solutions.

• Have goals oriented around a single process or area.

• Look at a particular issue to implement improvements.

## Kaizen Super Blitz

Kaizen Super Blitz are often times exercises carried out to fix any issues or wastes detected in business processes.

Kaizen Super Blitz often times,

• Are individual or group exercises involving workforce, and at times management.

• Take somewhere around 30 minutes to 8 hours.

• Focus on identifying and implementing immediate fixes and improvements.

• May involve little amount of study and analysis of problems and solutions.

• Have goals oriented around a single process or area.

• Look at a particular issue and implement improvements or fixes.

The figure below different Kaizen activities, for better understanding.

- Are group exercises involving workforce and management.
- Take somewhere between 5 to 7 days.
- Focus on establishing goals and plans to implement improvements.
- May involve significant study and analysis of problems and solutions.
- Establish goals oriented around multiple processes or areas.
- Focus on different aspects of the business.

- Are group exercises involving workforce and management.
- Take somewhere around 5 days.
- Focus on identifying and implementing significant process improvements.
- May involve significant study and analysis of problems and solutions.
- Have goals oriented around a single process or area.
- Loot at a particular issue to implement improvements.

- Are individual or group exercises involving workforce and management.
- Take somewhere around 2 to 5 days.
- Focus on identifying and implementing minor process improvements.
- May involve some amount of study and analysis of problems and solutions.
- Have Goals oriented around a single process or area.
- Loot at a particular issue to implement improvements.

- Are individual or group exercises involving workforce, and at times management.
- Take somewhere around 30 minutes to 8 hours.
- Focus on identifying and implementing immediate fixes and improvements.
- May involve little amount of study and analysis of problems and solutions.
- Have goals oriented around a single process or area.
- Look at a particular issue and implement improvements or fixes.

The figure below depicts different Kaizen activities based on the effort and time, for better understanding.

# KAIZEN MINDSET

For Kaizen to be successful, businesses should foster what is known as the **Kaizen Mindset**.

Kaizen mindset is a thought process that compels the workforce to always seek out continuous improvements in each and everything they do.

Kaizen mindset is the ideology that thinks,

• Everything can be improved, and hence should be.

• Improvement should happen each and everyday.

• Think as a customer as you provide their needs.

• Stop criticizing and start improving.

• Stop thinking why something can't be improved and start thinking how it can be.

• Set self targets and achieve them.

- Let competition inspire and interest you.

- Stop working for rewards.

- Question more.

- Trust, believe and always say "I can do it".

The figure below depicts different Kaizen ideologies that make up a Kaizen Mindeset.

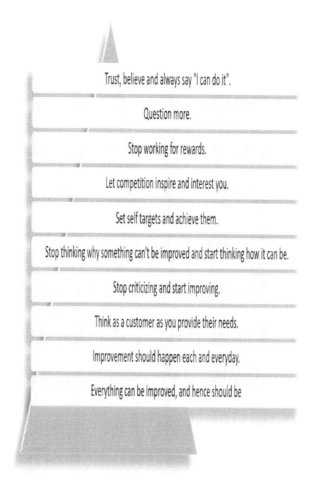

Trust, believe and always say "I can do it".

Question more.

Stop working for rewards.

Let competition inspire and interest you.

Set self targets and achieve them.

Stop thinking why something can't be improved and start thinking how it can be.

Stop criticizing and start improving.

Think as a customer as you provide their needs.

Improvement should happen each and everyday.

Everything can be improved, and hence should be

# KAIZEN SUGGESTION SYSTEM

For Kaizen to be successful, once the **Kaizen Mindset** is fostered in the workforce, the next step is to empower them to contribute improvement ideas.

This is where the **Kaizen Suggestion System** comes into picture.

Kaizen Suggestion system is a system which encourages the workforce to contribute process improvement ideas, which will be evaluated, implemented, and recognized.

The basic idea is to convert a complaining workforce to thinking, engaging, and contributing workforce, and to foster participation

The Kaizen Suggestion System most often works as follows,

• Whenever people from the workforce face a problem, they will think of ways to improve the problem and submit their process improvement ideas.

• These ideas will be evaluated for feasibility, return on investment, and other factors.

• Approved ideas will be implemented and benefits achieved.

• People contributing the implemented ideas will be recognized and awarded, to encourage further participation from the entire workforce.

The figure below depicts Kaizen Suggestion System in action.

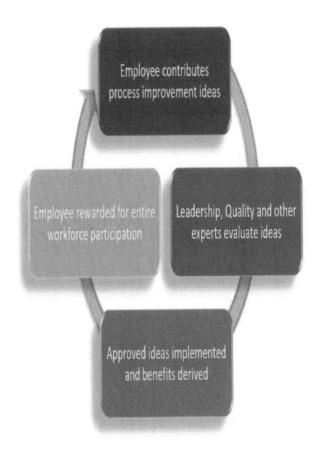

# KAIZEN CIRCLE

For Kaizen to be successful, once the **Kaizen Mindset** and **Kaizen Suggestion System** are in place, the next step is to encourage, drive, and govern the continuous improvements in business.

This is where the **Kaizen Circle** comes into picture.

Kaizen Circle is a group of members who come together voluntarily to help drive and govern the processes for identifying improvement opportunities, finding out root causes, identifying solutions and implementing them.

The Kaizen Circle members meet regularly at a decided frequency to ensure the continuous improvement initiatives are happening and achieving success as expected.

The Kaizen Circles most often work with an aim to,

• Foster team spirit in the workforce.

- Bring out a sense of belonging in the workplace.

- Improve and sustain quality in the business processes and products.

- Encourage workforce to contribute improvement ideas.

- Promote self participation in the workforce.

- Educate the workforce in techniques of executing improvement projects.

- Govern the improvement projects, workshops, and events are conducted in the right way and spirit.

The figure below depicts different Kaizen Circle goals, for better understanding.

# KAIZEN CULTURE

For Kaizen to be successful, an environment for it to succeed and foster needs to be created.

This is where the **Kaizen Culture** comes into picture.

**Kaizen Mindset**, **Kaizen Suggestion System** and **Kaizen Circles** are the major components of a **Kaizen Culture**. We have discussed them in previous chapters

Apart from these a few more things are a must to foster a Kaizen Culture.

They are,

• **Leadership and Management Commitment and Support,** For any business initiative to be successful, leadership and management's commitment and support are a must. The business leadership should always display how important the continuous improvements are for them, for the business, and for the workforce. Only if the management can establish themselves as role models can the workforce be inspired and participate.

• **Customer orientation,** Businesses exist to satisfy the needs of customer by providing high quality value products and services. So customer orientation is a must to ensure the process improvements are focusing on creating or increasing value to the customer.

• **Disciplined approach,** Process improvements use up costs, and resources. It is a must that the process improvements are happening in alignment to the business. Else it may so happen that the workforce is working towards process improvements, however they are not the processes which the business may have any interest in.

• **Kaizen process**, The final most important component of a Kaizen culture is the Kaizen process, or a step by step methodology to implement Kaizen improvements. We are going to look at the Kaizen process in the next section in detail.

The figure below depicts components of the Kaizen Culture for better understanding.

# KAIZEN PROCESS

# KAIZEN PDCA

Most often Kaizen are executed as PDCA projects or cycles, also known as Deming's Cycles. Where P stands for Plan, D for Do, C for Check, and A for Act.

The essential activities carried out in a **Kaizen PDCA** project are,

• **Plan**, Involves assessing the process that needs to be improved, or a new process that needs to be developed, and focuses on brainstorming ways to improve the process to put up an improvement plan.

• **Do,** Involves executing the established plan, collecting the data to study, and developing and testing the improvement solution.

• **Check**, Involves analyzing the collected data, evaluating and comparing against the established standards or the target, to assess the improvement.

• **Act,** Involves base-lining and establishing the new improved process.

**Case Study:** To understand the Kaizen PDCA process in action, lets take a very simple everyday business case study of creating a report and sending it to management. Most often the reports we create on regular basis have multiple data sources from which we pull the data, convert it into meaningful information, put it in an excel or word or presentation file, format the file and send across to the management.

The figure below depicts the Kaizen PDCA cycle for better understanding.

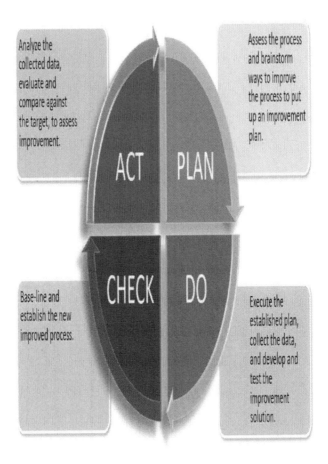

# Essential activities of Kaizen PDCA

The essential activities carried out in a **Kaizen PDCA** project are,

## Plan.

• Prepare Business Case.

• Frame Problem Statement.

• Frame Goal Statement.

• Establish Scope.

• Form Project Team.

• Establish Time lines.

• Calculate AS IS Data.

• Plan Solution.

## Do.

• Develop and Test Solution.

• Calculate TO BE Data.

## Check.

• Perform Data Review.

• Calculate Realization.

## Act.

• Develop Action Plan.

• Establish Future Milestones.

The figure below depicts the essential activities of the Kaizen PDCA cycle for better understanding.

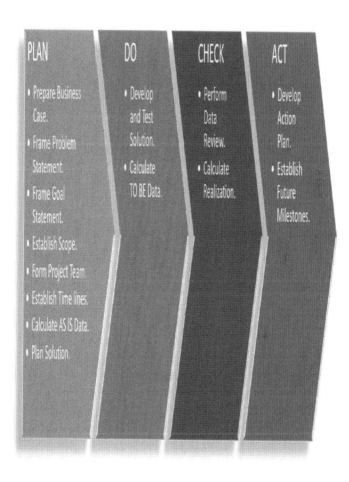

# KAIZEN PLAN PHASE

## Prepare Business Case

A Business Case is a concise description of the improvement opportunity, explaining in brief the problem, the goal of the Kaizen event, the reason why the Kaizen event is important, along with financial justification if any for the execution of the Kaizen event, and most importantly what is the negative impact, if the Kaizen event is not executed right now.

You may want to prepare the business case document, to enable the sponsor or the management decide whether they can approve the Kaizen opportunity for execution, over other potential improvement opportunities.

**Example:** "ABC Business's Sales Analytic Team performs daily monitoring, reporting sales activity of their XYZ product range.

The report captures the details of daily sales of their

various XYZ products on their e portal, including the product ID, product name, sale date and quantity.

• The Sales analytic team fetches details required for the report.

• Creates an excel report.

• And sends to the Business lead.

Daily there are at least around 50 product varieties sold for which the data needs to be fetched.

Fetching the details, formatting the data into an excel report, and sending to the Business Lead takes around 2 hours daily, amounting to 47,450 USD annually.

This Kaizen event aims at reducing this manual effort wastage by at least 80% and achieving a dollar saving of at least 37960 USD.

If this Kaizen event is not initiated right now, it will result in continued wastage of effort and productivity."

## Frame Problem Statement

A Problem Statement is a concise description of the problem or the issue or the condition which the Kaizen PDCA project focuses to improve.

You may want to prepare the problem statement, to help management and other stakeholders identify the gap between the current and desired states of a process or product, and understand why the Kaizen PDCA project or the Kaizen event is being executed.

**Example:** "ABC Business's Sales Analytic Team performs daily monitoring, reporting sales activity of their XYZ product range.

The report captures the details of daily sales of their various XYZ products on their e portal, including the product ID, product name, sale date and quantity.

• The Sales analytic team fetches the product sold within the last 24 hour, along with their 'ID', and 'Name' from the XYZ product database.

• Then it fetches sale date, including the time, and quantity for all these products from e portal system.

• The Sales Support team then puts the data into an excel file, formats it.

• And then emails this excel report to the Business Lead.

Daily there are at least around 50 products sold for which the data needs to be fetched.

Fetching the details from multiple sources and formatting the data into an excel takes around 2 hours daily.

This amounts to 47,450 USD annually at 65 USD hourly rate, and is a huge expense and productivity loss."

## Frame Goal Statement

A Goal Statement is a concise description of the goal or the aim or the desired state which the Kaizen PDCA project or the Kaizen event focuses to achieve within the specified period of time.

You may want to frame the goal statement, to help the stakeholders identify the desired state of a process or product, the improvement target, and the deadline for the project.

And may need to keep the goal statement SMART (Specific, Measurable, Attainable, Relevant, Time bound)

**Example:** "Reduce the manual effort spent creating the daily sales analysis report by at least 80% by 31st August 2018, resulting in annual saving of at least 37960 USD."

## Establish Scope

Scope is a concise description clearly demarcating what is in scope and what is out of scope of the Kaizen PDCA project or the Kaizen event.

You may want to establish the scope, to keep the team focused, and to set clear expectations for the stakeholders, in terms of what will be covered by the event.

### Example:

In scope:

ABC Business

XYZ products Daily Sales Report

Out scope:

Anything beyond

## Form Project Team

While forming a team to execute the Kaizen PDCA project it is important to pick up employees who are close to and involved in the process, as they know the process and its issues the best.

You may want to establish the project team, identify their roles, and also identify any other important stakeholders who may contribute to the success of the Kaizen project.

### Example:

Developers: Suneet K

Testers: Mitali S and Manali S

Implementation: Yashwant K

Product Owner: Sahana KS

Coach and Mentor: Sumeet S

## Establish Timelines

Timelines is a concise description clearly mentioning the timelines needed for completion of the entire project, as well as for each phase of the Kaizen PDCA project or the Kaizen event.

You may want to establish the timelines, to keep the team focused, and to set clear expectations for the stakeholders, in terms of the deadlines to meet.

**Example:**

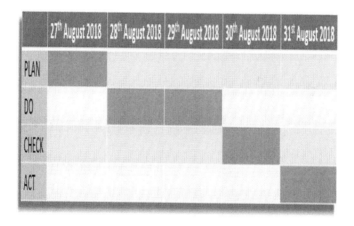

|  | 27th August 2018 | 28th August 2018 | 29th August 2018 | 30th August 2018 | 31st August 2018 |
|---|---|---|---|---|---|
| PLAN |  |  |  |  |  |
| DO |  |  |  |  |  |
| CHECK |  |  |  |  |  |
| ACT |  |  |  |  |  |

SUMEET SAVANT

## Calculate AS IS Data

AS IS Data is a concise description describing the performance of the AS IS process derived from the data collected.

You may want to collect the AS IS Data, to understand the current or AS IS performance.

**Example:**

| Reading No. | Effort in min to fetch data and create report | Reading No. | Effort in min to fetch data and create report |
|---|---|---|---|
| 1 | 120 | 14 | 119 |
| 2 | 118 | 15 | 120 |
| 3 | 119 | 16 | 122 |
| 4 | 121 | 17 | 117 |
| 5 | 122 | 18 | 119 |
| 6 | 123 | 19 | 120 |
| 7 | 121 | 20 | 118 |
| 8 | 120 | 21 | 119 |
| 9 | 119 | 22 | 120 |
| 10 | 120 | 23 | 123 |
| 11 | 117 | 24 | 120 |
| 12 | 123 | 25 | 125 |
| 13 | 122 | | |

**Effort Mean: 120 minutes**

102

## Plan Solution

Planning solution activity includes figuring out root causes, coming up with few solutions, selecting a solution, and designing the selected solution.

You may want to plan the solution, to address the right root causes, select the best possible solution, and design the solution in the best possible way.

Tools like Fish Bone Analysis, Control Impact Matrix. Flow charts and others will be useful here.

### Example:

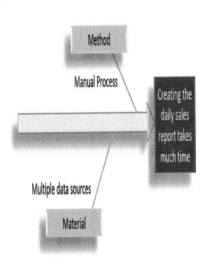

| | High Impact | Low Impact |
|---|---|---|
| In Control | Manual Process | |
| Not In Control | Multiple Data Sources | |

# KAIZEN DO PHASE

## Develop and Test Solution

Developing and testing solution activity includes developing the solution based on the design planned and testing the solution.

You may want to develop the solution in the best possible way, and develop test cases to verify and validate the working of the solution, before going live.

### Example:

| SL No. | Description | Expected Result | Observed Result |
|---|---|---|---|
| 1 | Fetching products sold | All relevant products sold are fetched | Same as expected |
| 2 | Fetch product ID, Name, and date | Product ID, Name, and date fetched as needed for the report | Same as expected |
| 3 | Report creation | Report created same as manual report sent to management | Same as expected |
| 4 | Report email | Report emailed automatically to management | Same as expected |

Use Java to automate fetching products sold

Use Java to automate fetching products id, name, and date

Use Java to automate creating the report from data fetched

Use Java to automate fetching to email report to management

## Calculate TO BE Data

TO BE Data is a concise description describing the performance of the AS IS process derived from the data collected.

You may want to collect the TO BE Data, to understand the improved performance.

**Example:**

| Reading No. | Effort in min to fetch data and create report | Reading No. | Effort in min to fetch data and create report |
|---|---|---|---|
| 1 | 7 | 14 | 5 |
| 2 | 6 | 15 | 6 |
| 3 | 6 | 16 | 7 |
| 4 | 7 | 17 | 6 |
| 5 | 8 | 18 | 6 |
| 6 | 7 | 19 | 7 |
| 7 | 5 | 20 | 6 |
| 8 | 6 | 21 | 7 |
| 9 | 5 | 22 | 6 |
| 10 | 6 | 23 | 7 |
| 11 | 5 | 24 | 6 |
| 12 | 7 | 25 | 6 |
| 13 | 6 | | |

**Effort Mean: 6.24 minutes**

# KAIZEN CHECK PHASE

## Perform Data Review

Data review is a concise description describing the comparison of the performance of AS IS and TO BE process based on the collected data, preferably in a visually enhanced manner.

You may want to perform data review, to evaluate the effectiveness and success of the executed Kaizen PDCA or the Kaizen event.

### Example:

Effort Before Kaizen - 120 minutes

Effort After Kaizen - 6.24 minutes

Effort Reduction Achieved - 94.8% i.e. 113.76 min saved

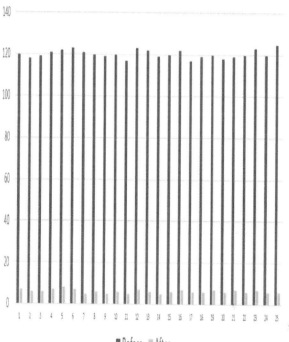

## Calculate Realization

Realization is a concise description clearly explaining the achievements of the executed Kaizen PDCA project.

You may want to calculate the realization, to summarize the overall achievements of the executed Kaizen PDCA project or the Kaizen event.

### Example:

Effort saved from 120 minutes to 6.24 minutes i.e. 94.8%.

Annual dollar spent before PDCA: 120 minutes * 365 days * 65 USD/60 minutes = 47450 USD

Annual dollar spent after PDCA: 6.24 minutes * 365 days * 65 USD/60 minutes = 2467.4 USD

Annual dollar saving achieved: 47450 USD – 2467 USD = 44983 USD.

# KAIZEN ACT PHASE

## Develop Action Plan

Action Plan is a concise description clearly explaining the plan of action devised in the ACT phase based on the achievements and realization summarized in the CHECK phase.

You may want to develop the action plan, to define the actions to be taken which can be either the steps taken to establish the developed solution as the new baseline, or to initiate a new Kaizen PDCA project or Kaizen event, or to fix the developed solution to use it as the new baseline.

### Example:

Educate the XYZ Sales Analytic team to use new solution by 31st August 2018.

Inform all stakeholders about the new baselined process by 31st August 2018.

Stop the old process and start using the new process by 1st September 2018.

## Establish Future Milestones

Future Milestones are a concise description clearly explaining any future milestones of new projects arising out of the executed Kaizen PDCA project or Kaizen event.

You may want to establish the future milestones, to help identify any new projects or events as a byproduct of the executed Kaizen PDCA project or event.

### Example:

Any next project(s) planned - Yes.

Need for next project(s) - Continuous Improvement.

Description – Automation of similar processes on the floor.

Timelines – End of December 2018.

Important Stakeholders and Team – Same as current project.

# AUTHOR'S NOTE

I thank you for choosing the book, I have presented to you a detailed approach towards executing a value stream mapping exercise.

I hope this adds value to you and helps you eliminate wastes, and achieve cost reductions in your processes.

**Please leave a review** wherever you bought the book, and it will help me in my quest to provide good useful products to you on Lean Six Sigma.

All the very best,

Sumeet Savant
 Lean Six Sigma Master Black Belt and Coach